Bienvenue Bukasa Muepu
Pierre Kafunda
Theodore Kabangu

Artificial learning based on convolution neural networks

Bienvenue Bukasa Muepu
Pierre Kafunda
Theodore Kabangu

Artificial learning based on convolution neural networks

Application to the recognition of handwritten digits on bank cheques

ScienciaScripts

Imprint
Any brand names and product names mentioned in this book are subject to trademark, brand or patent protection and are trademarks or registered trademarks of their respective holders. The use of brand names, product names, common names, trade names, product descriptions etc. even without a particular marking in this work is in no way to be construed to mean that such names may be regarded as unrestricted in respect of trademark and brand protection legislation and could thus be used by anyone.

Cover image: www.ingimage.com

This book is a translation from the original published under ISBN 978-620-6-70491-1.

Publisher:
Sciencia Scripts
is a trademark of
Dodo Books Indian Ocean Ltd. and OmniScriptum S.R.L publishing group

120 High Road, East Finchley, London, N2 9ED, United Kingdom
Str. Armeneasca 28/1, office 1, Chisinau MD-2012, Republic of Moldova, Europe
Managing Directors: Ieva Konstantinova, Victoria Ursu
info@omniscriptum.com

Printed at: see last page
ISBN: 978-620-8-57821-3

INTRODUCTION

Artificial learning has made it possible to build models that enable machines to learn and train themselves on the basis of examples, so that they can evolve autonomously. Over the last few decades, we have seen a great deal of progress in a number of areas, including medicine, industry, banking systems and so on.

With the advent of pattern recognition, artificial learning can be integrated into computer systems to give them the ability to simulate the human activities of perception, recognition and understanding, such as recognising objects, writing and speech. Computers have thus been able to acquire a high level of understanding from digital images or videos.

Image , the study of digital images and their transformations to improve quality and extract information, has been the subject of much research in recent years. Computer systems capable of perceiving, recognising and understanding information on an image exploit recent machine learning techniques, especially deep learning. These include convolutional neural networks, whose success in image processing remains far superior to that of simple artificial neural networks.

In this work, we will apply convolutional neural networks to image processing of bank cheques to give the computer the ability to recognise the amounts written by humans so that this information can be used to process cheque transactions. Today, handwriting recognition, a sub-domain of pattern recognition, has demonstrated a certain success in a number of activities, such as the automatic sorting of mail in the post office and the reading of cheque amounts in a bank, to name but a few. Applied to handwritten figures in the banking sector, its purpose is to convert the image of a character that can be understood by humans into a code that can be interpreted by a computer. However, it is much more complex for handwritten characters because of the extreme variability of the latter: variability of shapes, spacing between words and characters, fluctuation of lines.

During cheque banking transactions, the amounts written on cheques need to be considered carefully. Error being human, a simple inattention to the amount can be the cause of an unexpected addition or deletion operation that may well be unfortunate for the bank or the customer. The credibility and profitability of the bank on the one hand, and the satisfaction of the customer on the other, are at stake. In view of the number of bank transactions involving cheques, it is a fact that repetition of such an error, to the detriment of the bank, is almost inevitable when humans are involved in this processing. Although unpredictable, the loss of earnings for the bank remains a considerable threat.

Faced with this situation, our thinking turned to the following questions:

✓ How can a computer system recognise the handwritten figures on a cheque?

✓ What contribution could an automatic handwriting recognition system make to banks?

In consideration of these research questions, different solutions may be proposed depending on the researcher. For us, in relation to the first question, we thought that handwritten digits would be recognised using a predictive model based on convolutional neural networks.

In relation to the second question, we believe that such a system could offer accuracy in entering the amount, and therefore speed in processing cheque transactions.

To present our solution, we have chosen the following theme: "**Artificial learning based on convolution neural networks for the recognition of handwritten digits in the case of bank cheques**".

In terms of this theme, this work is of no less interest. In fact, it has enabled us understand deep automatic learning, pattern recognition and more.

character recognition and computer vision. For banks, this work is helping to improve their quality of service and speed up cheque transaction processing. For future researchers, the work is intended as a reference for those tackling the subject of convolutional neural networks and optical character recognition.

The aim of this work is to build, train and optimise a model based on a convolutional neural network, capable of recognising the handwritten digits written on a cheque. To achieve this objective, we used the descriptive method, which enabled us to describe the character recognition process. The experimental method enabled us to experiment with digit recognition using the MNIST dataset. The documentary technique enabled us to gain an insight into the organisation of the learning base into pixel values.

In time, our work will be carried out during the 2020-2021 academic year. Our study is aimed at recognising handwritten numbers, and we have limited ourselves to building the model, training it, testing it and optimising it. The system can classify the image on the basis of its pixel values, but it has not yet reached the point of acquiring an external image and converting it into pixels.

With the exception of the introduction and general conclusion, the bulk of this work will be divided into the following sections four main chapters:

Chapter I: Artificial learning; in this chapter, we present the computer science field in which our work is situated and some key concepts relating to this field.

Chapter II: Pattern recognition; in this chapter, we give an overview of pattern recognition and the steps taken to build a handwriting recognition system.

Chapter III: Convolutional neural networks; this chapter is devoted to the description convolutional neural networks and their place in the field of classification.

Chapter IV: Implementation and interpretation of results; this chapter deals with the experimental part of our work and the presentation of the results obtained.

CHAPTER I

ARTIFICIAL LEARNING

I.1. Introduction

Man is a creature of concern for several disciplines because of the needs he expresses. One of these needs is to learn, in order to inform and educate ourselves through the performance of our moral, physical, spiritual and intellectual capacities. Learning takes many forms: learning by instruction, by extrapolation, by discovery, by training, whether supervised or autonomous. But today, thanks to the rapid development of computer science, machines can also learn. The aim of this so-called artificial machine learning is to enable machines to understand natural phenomena. But this understanding is based on the construction of models that must be capable of running simulations. In this chapter we will define the concepts of Machine Learning and explain the types of learning used in automatic learning. We will also define Deep Learning, which is a branch of Machine Learning.

I.2. Definitions [12]

Artificial learning is one of the fields of study of artificial intelligence. It is the scientific discipline concerned with the development, analysis and implementation of automatable methods that enable a machine (in the broadest sense) to evolve through a learning process, and thus to perform tasks that are difficult or impossible to perform by more conventional algorithmic means.

Artificial learning, a science that seeks and establishes links between the general principles of learning and the methods and tools that enable learning to take place in a particular context.

Machine learning is now an important component of several fields such as automatic natural language processing, object recognition, speech recognition, bioinformatics and many others. It is itself a discipline at the intersection of several others, as shown in the figure below.

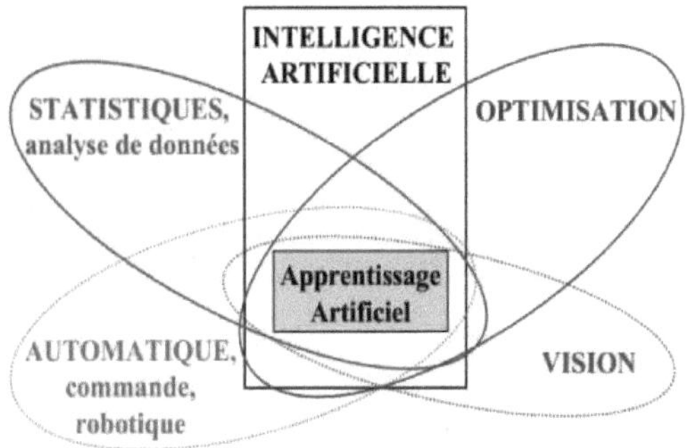

Figure I.1: The multidisciplinary nature of Machine Learning [MINES ParisTech May 2011].

I.3. Principle and Objectives of Machine Learning [9]

Machine learning is defined by the construction of models. This is done using an algorithmic approach. The algorithms used enable, to a certain extent, a computer-controlled (possibly a robot) or computer-assisted system to adapt its analyses and behaviour in response, based on the analysis of empirical data from a database or sensors.

However, the difficulty lies in the fact that the set of all possible behaviours given all possible inputs quickly becomes too complex to describe (known as a combinatorial explosion). We therefore entrust programmes with the task of adjusting a model to simplify this complexity and use it operationally. In addition, the model must be adaptive, in that it must take account of changes in the information base for which the response behaviours have been validated, which is what constitutes learning; this enables the analysis or response system to improve itself. Ideally, learning aims to be unsupervised, meaning that the nature of the training data is not known. Machine Learning is a vast and complex field with so many objectives:

✓ Write computer programmes that are likely to improve automatically over time, either on the basis of their own experience or from previous data provided by other programmes;

✓ Predict behaviour in the face of new data and approximate a function or probability density;

✓ Automatically extract and exploit information from a dataset;

✓ Confirm hypotheses proposed by decision-makers and analysts and provide them with a confidence level ;

✓ Equipping system computers artificial or automatic learning modules;

I.4. Learning

Depending on the domain, knowledge or learning data can take various forms: words, phrases, variables or attributes, vectors of values defining a set of properties of an object. Learning data is often divided into 3 categories:

✓ The training set or training population: this is the set of candidates or examples (images, attributes) used to generate the training model. ;

✓ The test set consists of the candidates to which the learning model will be applied (to test and correct the algorithm);

✓ The validation set can be used during training (as a sub-population of the training set) to validate (integrate) the model and avoid over-learning.

I.5. Key terms

Among the main concepts essential to Machine Learning we can cite and define:

✓ Dataset: This is a set of values where each value is associated with a variable and an observation. In Machine Learning, everything starts with a dataset containing our data. In supervised learning, the dataset contains the questions (x) and answers (y) to the problem that the machine must solve.

✓ The model and its parameters: From this dataset, we create a model, which is nothing more than a mathematical function. The coefficients of this function are the model parameters.

✓ The Cost Function: When we test our model on the dataset, it gives us errors. All these errors are called the Cost Function.

✓ The Learning : The central idea of Machine Learning is to let the

machine to find the parameters of our model that minimise the Cost Function.

I.6. Types of machine learning

There are several types of learning system, and they vary according to the type of problem being . It is therefore useful to classify them into different categories. Machine Learning systems can be classified according to the extent and nature of the supervision they require during the training phase. There are four main categories: supervised learning, unsupervised learning, semi-supervised learning and reinforcement learning.

I.6.1. **Supervised learning** [26] [2]

Supervised learning is perhaps the easiest type of Machine Learning problem to grasp: its aim is to learn how to make predictions, based on a list of labelled examples, i.e. accompanied by the value to be predicted. The labels act as a "teacher" and supervise the learning of the algorithm.The branch of machine learning known as supervised learning is concerned with problems that can be formalised as follows: given n observations {~x i}i=1,...,n described in a space X , and their labels {y i}i=1,...,n described in a space Y, we assumes that labels can be obtained from observations using a fixed and unknown function φ : X → Y: y i = φ(~x i) + i , where i is random noise. The task is then to use the data to determine a function f : X → Y such that, for any pair (~x, φ(~x)) E X × Y, f(~x) ≈ φ(~x).

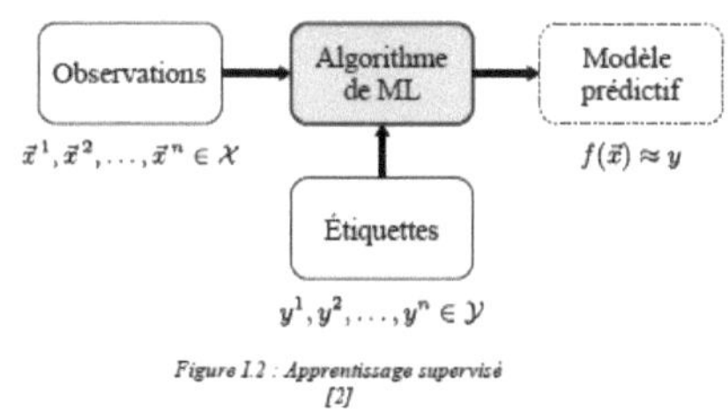

Figure I.2: Supervised learning [2].

Another important categorisation in machine learning, linked to the very nature of the targets, is the type of problem to be solved. We will present the two types most commonly used in the literature. These are targets composed of discrete or continuous values.

a) Classification

Typically, for a classification problem, the dataset used has a finite number of classes and each example is associated with one of them. The target of each example will have a discrete value representing a particular class. With such data, a machine learning will learn to assign classes to inputs.

Typical examples include the recognition of a simple number in an image, the fact that a customer belongs to a customer segment or may be part of a particular type of customer (dissatisfied, likely to unsubscribe to a service, etc.) or the detection of a virus based on the behaviour or characteristics of a software application.

b) Regression

In a regression problem, the target is made up of one or more elements with continuous values. A machine learning model will learn to predict one or more real values. In meteorology, temperature prediction is a good example of a regression problem. In this case, the value to be predicted is continuous. Other elements can also be added to the target, such as atmospheric pressure and humidity, creating a vector of continuous values.

c) Supervised learning

There are several supervised learning algorithms:

- ✓ The K nearest neighbours
- ✓ Support vector machines
- ✓ Decision trees
- ✓ Neural networks

I.6.2. Unsupervised learning [25] [2]

Unsupervised learning consists of highlighting information hidden the large volume of data, with a view to detecting hidden trends in the data. In this case, the data is not labelled, and there are no hypotheses or additional information about the data. In other words, the classes are not known and must be determined. Unsupervised learning is the branch of Machine Learning that deals with problems that can be formalised as follows: given n observations {~x ^{i}}i=1,...,n described in a space X, we need to learn a function on X that verifies certain properties.

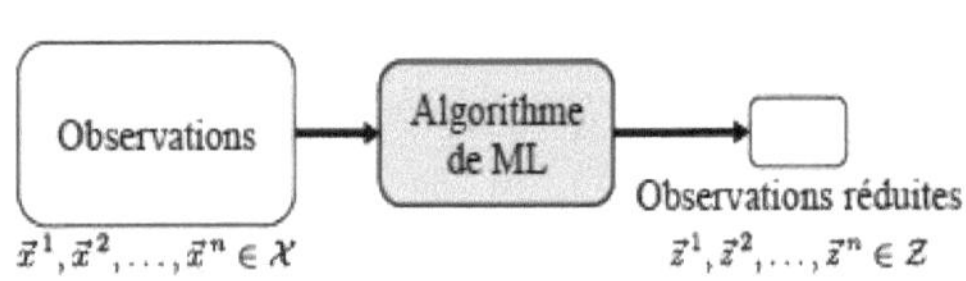

Figure I.3: Unsupervised learning [2].

a) Applications

The problem to be solved by the f(x) function is therefore defined by the user. However, whatever the problem chosen, an unsupervised model will always learn features related to the probability distribution generating the training data. There are many problems in unsupervised learning:

✓ Feature extraction: The learned function f(x) provides a new representation for the input x. In general, this representation is used to perform another task for which it is more useful than the original input.

✓ Density estimation: The function f(x) must estimate the probability distribution of the examples of the drive assembly.

✓ Clustering: In the space containing the training set data, the learning must identify groupings of distinct examples. We obtain a function f(x) which provides the index of the cluster associated with example x.

✓ Dimensionality reduction: As with feature extraction, the function f(x) must provide a new representation for the input x. However, the aim this time is obtain a representation with a smaller dimensionality than that of the input, while retaining the important information.

b) Unsupervised learning

There are several algorithms, such as :

- ✓ K-means (KMeans)
- ✓ Hierarchical grouping
- ✓ Fuzzy c-means

I.6.3. Semi-supervised learning [2]

Semi-supervised learning consists of learning labels from a partially labelled dataset. The first advantage of this approach is that it avoids having to label all the training examples, which is relevant when it is easy to accumulate data but labelling them requires a certain amount of human work.

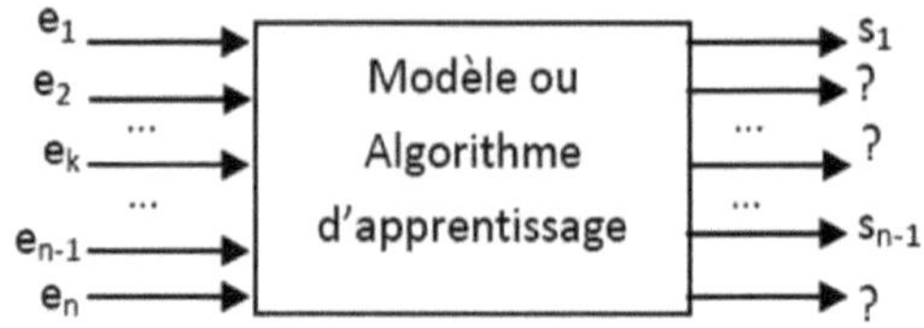

Figure I.4: Semi-supervised learning

I.6.4. **Reinforcement learning** [2]

In reinforcement learning, the learning system can interact with its environment and perform actions. In return for these actions, it obtains a reward, which may be positive if the action was a good choice, or negative if it was not. The reward can sometimes come after a long series of actions; this is the case, for example, for a system learning to play Go or chess. In this case, learning consists of defining a policy, i.e. a strategy for systematically obtaining the best possible reward. The main applications of reinforcement learning are in games (chess, go, etc) and robotics.

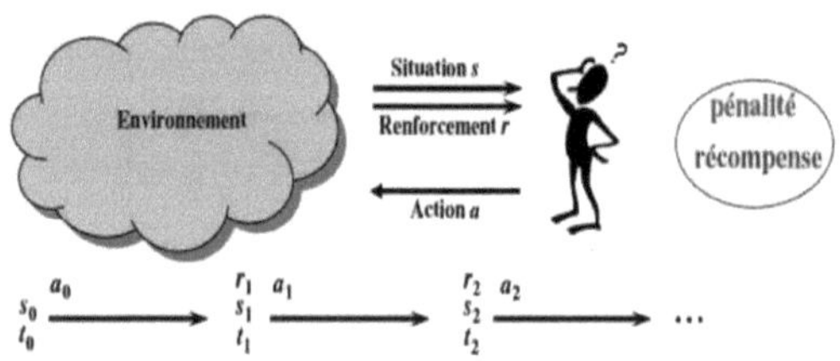

Figure I.5: Reinforcement learning

I.7. Fields of application for Machine Learning

Among the many areas application artificial learning, we can mention :

- ✓ Handwriting recognition
- ✓ Medical diagnosis
- ✓ Search engines
- ✓ Autonomous driving
- ✓ Computer vision

✓ Robotics

✓ Analysing and understanding images

✓ Pattern recognition

I.8. Deep Learning [9]

I.8.1. Introduction

Deep Learning is a discipline of artificial intelligence, and more specifically a branch of Machine Learning. It involves letting machines learn from their own experience, in the same way as humans.

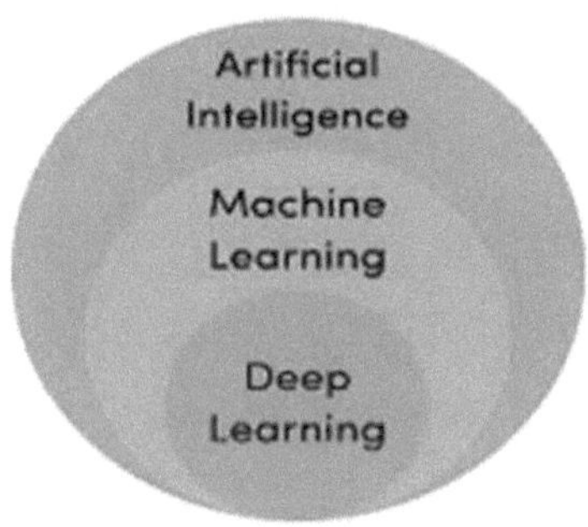

Figure I.6 : Relationship between artificial intelligence, machine learning and deep learning [https://f.hubspotusercontent10.net/hubfs/636866/Blog/FR/FR%20Blog%20Inside%20Images/IAvs-ML-DL.png]

The artificial neural networks on which Deep Learning is based learn by discovering structures in the data provided to them. These networks develop calculation models made up of multiple layers of processing, in order to create multiple levels of abstraction to represent the data.A Deep Learning model of the convolutional neural network type can be trained on millions of images of cats. It will then learn to recognise the pixels representing a cat, in order to classify them as such. With a conventional Machine Learning system, a human expert would have to spend a considerable amount of time configuring the system to enable it to detect the characteristics of the cat. In the case of Deep Learning, all it needs is a large quantity of images. Deep Learning algorithms outperform Machine Learning systems in a large number of tasks, including computer vision, speech recognition and robotics. However, hyperparameters need to be configured for the model to be effective.

Deep Learning is used for a wide variety applications, such as detecting disease, inspecting industrial equipment, autonomous vehicles, discovering exoplanets or medicines, studying the genome or combating global warming.

I.8.2. How Deep Learning works [18]

Deep Learning is based on a network of artificial neurons inspired by the human brain. This network is made up of dozens or even hundreds of layers of neurons, each receiving and interpreting information from the previous layer.

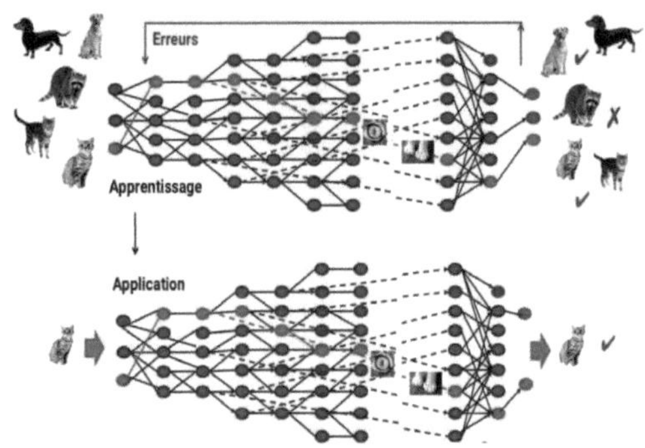

Figure I.7: The process of learning and identifying a cat using deep learning [https://www.futura-sciences.com/tech/definitions/intelligence-artificielle-deep-learning17262/]

At each stage, the wrong answers are eliminated and sent back upstream to adjust the mathematical model. As it goes along, the programme reorganises the information into more complex blocks. When this model is subsequently applied to other cases, it is normally able to recognise a cat without anyone ever telling it that it has never learned the concept of a cat. The initial data is essential, and the more different experiences the system accumulates, the better it will perform.

I.8.3. Deep Learning algorithm

There are a large number of variants of deep architectures. Most of them are derived from some of the original parent architectures. It is not always possible to compare the performance of all the architectures, as they are not all evaluated on the same data sets. Deep Learning is a fast-growing field, and new architectures, variants or algorithms appear every week. There are various Deep Learning algorithms:

✓ Recurrent Neural Networks (RNN)

✓ Generative Adversarial Networks (GAN)

✓ Convolutional Neural Networks (CNN)

Convolutional neural networks (CNNs) and their different layers will be explained more detail in another chapter.

I.8.4. Application of Deep Learning

Deep Learning is used in many fields:

✓ Image recognition

✓ Machine translation

✓ Personalised recommendations

✓ Space exploration

✓ Fraud detection

I.9. Conclusion

The various algorithms used in ML emerged during the 20th century. For years, neural networks were consigned to oblivion. The recent emergence of Deep Learning, which is a branch of Machine Learning, is due to the development of GPUs and the availability of large quantities of data. It's fair to say that this technology has been ahead of its time. Deep Learning has many applications in all fields, from voice processing to pattern recognition. The next chapter will focus on computer pattern recognition, which is essential to this project.

CHAPTER II

PATTERN RECOGNITION

II.1. Introduction

Every day, human beings intuitively perform the task of distinguishing between objects of known shape. For these simple tasks, humans are considered to be relatively perfect systems compared with artificial recognition systems.However, recognition becomes very difficult and requires more effort and time in other cases, such as: reading the amounts of cheques, addresses, letters to classify them according to city, searching a huge database of fingerprints to judge a suspect, determining the identity a speaker from his or her voice. Automatic pattern recognition is making a comeback, not to replace humans with machines, but to relieve them of critical and tedious tasks. This chapter begins with a general presentation of pattern , outlining the general framework and typical areas of application. The chapter ends with a brief description of each stage in the general scheme of a handwriting recognition .

II.2. Overview of pattern recognition [5] [24] [6].

The concept of shape must be taken in a broader sense, not just that of geometric form but rather of patterns, which can be of various kinds. They can be visual (barcodes, faces, fingerprints, etc.), aural (speech), chemical (smell), multi-spectral (satellite images), and many others.

II.2.1. Definition

Pattern recognition (or RDF) is a field of artificial intelligence that makes it possible to create computerised systems capable of simulating the human activities of perception, recognition and comprehension: recognition of writing, speech, etc. It stems from different disciplines: mathematics (probability and statistics), engineering sciences and computer science. It draws on a number of disciplines, including mathematics (probability and statistics), engineering sciences and computer science.This discipline refers to methods which, based on the observation an object, enable it to be assign a specific class. For example, a system which, based on a radar observation, classifies flying objects into either an aircraft class or a non-aircraft class, performs a object recognition task.

II.2.2. Aim of pattern recognition

The aim of pattern recognition is to create computerised systems that simulate the human activities of perception, recognition and comprehension: recognition of writing, speech, scene interpretation and robotics. The problem that pattern recognition seeks to solve is associate a class with an unknown shape (which does not yet have an associated class). Pattern recognition is often seen as a classification problem: finding the function that assigns any unknown shape to its most relevant class.

II.2.3. Principle and formulation

The general principle of **RDF** is to classify new shapes using a classifier that generates a membership function for each class. In this way, a new point can be classified according to the membership value it obtains in relation to each class. Pattern recognition is performed in two phases: learning from known data and classification of new or unknown data. Prior to these two phases, a pre-processing stage is used to find the minimum set of informative parameters required to establish the representation space.

II.2.4. Some pattern recognition methods

Here we try to match the different ways of representing exemplars and classes and the different methods for learning and recognition. But they also correspond to different ways of approaching the problem of pattern recognition. We are interested here in the simulation of a human being in a recognition task, which does not cover all the problems dealt with by pattern recognition. The shapes sought can be well-known geometric shapes such as the circle, ellipse, triangle, polygon, rectangle, square, line, curve, straight line and complex shapes such as a retinal print, fingerprint, letter or number. There are several learning algorithms for pattern recognition:

- ✓ Bayesian method ;
- ✓ Linear classifier ;
- ✓ The Deep Learning algorithm ;
- ✓ Convolution neural networks ;
- ✓ Support Vector Machines ...etc.

In our work, we are only interested in pattern recognition using convolution neural networks.

II.2.5. Typical applications of pattern recognition

Generally speaking, the objects to be recognised are of the signal or image type, which implies two main factors families applications :

a) Signal recognition

This family tries automate the interpretation of signals:

- ✓ Voice signals automate a human's auditory behaviour:

speech recognition, speaker recognition ;

- ✓ Biomedical signals: electrocardiogram ;
- ✓ Instrument monitoring, fault diagnosis ;

b) Pattern recognition in digital images

In this family we are trying automate the process of human vision:

- ✓ Fingerprint recognition ;
- ✓ Handwriting recognition ;
- ✓ Document analysis ;
- ✓ Satellite imagery ;
- ✓ Scene analysis, image ;

II.3. Basics of image

II.3.1. Definition [22]

An image is a planar representation of a scene or object located in three-dimensional space. It can be described in the form a function I (x, y) where x and y are the spatial coordinates of a point in the image and I is a function of light intensity (grey level and colour). The information in an image is :

- ✓ Number of lines ;
- ✓ Number of columns ;

✓ Pixel format (bits, grey levels, colour levels) ;

✓ Possible compression ;

II.3.2. Scanning

Digitisation involves creating a digital copy of an original document in paper format that can be accessed and used online. An image can be represented by a two-dimensional matrix of numerical values f(x, y), where x, y are the Cartesian coordinates of a point in the image and f(x, y) gives the grey level at that point.In general, data is displayed and addressed in the form of an array, here called I, with n rows and p columns. Each element I(x, y) of this array represents a pixel in image. The value of this pixel will be associated with a grey level encoded on m bits (2^m grey levels; 0 = black; 1=white). The value at each point expresses the luminous intensity perceived by the sensor.

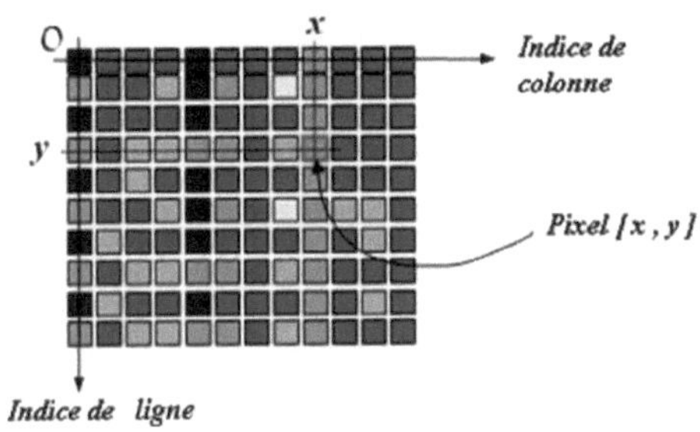

Figure II.1: Digital image

The image is saved in the form of a computer file containing :

✓ A name ;

✓ A 3-letter suffix (e.g. bmp, jpg, etc.) specifying the type of coding used.

II.3.3. Pixel [22] [13]

This is the smallest element used to define the base of a digital image. It represents a given point (x, y) in the image plane. The information presented by the pixel is the grey level (or colour) taken from the corresponding location in the real image. For a monochrome image, each pixel is coded on one byte. In a colour image (RGB), a pixel can be represented on three bytes, i.e. one byte for each of the primary colours: red (R), green (G) and blue (B).

II.3.4. Image size [13]

The size of an image corresponds to the number of points (or pixels) that make up the width and height of a digital image (the number of columns and the number of rows). This is also known as pixel size. Example: an image with a definition of 1600 x 1200 corresponds to an image 1600 pixels wide and 1200 pixels high. We also know that 100 pixels = 1 inch = 25.4mm.

II.3.5. Different formats

a) Raster image

A raster image (or bitmap) is made up of an array of points or pixels. Each dot carries position and colour information. The higher the dot density, the greater the amount of information and the higher the resolution of the image. The images seen on a television screen or in a photograph are raster images.

b) Vector image

A vector image is a digital image made up of several individual geometric objects (lines, polygons, arcs of circles). In a vector image, the data is represented using mathematical formulae. This allows the image to be enlarged indefinitely with no loss of quality and a small footprint.

II.3.6. Colour coding

There are 3 main types of colour in a digital image:

- ✓ Black and white image coding ;
- ✓ Image coding in greyscale ;
- ✓ Colour image coding ;

These types are generally selected scanning with a scanner or when using the configuration.

a) Coding a black and white image

The simplest image coding is black and white. In this type of coding, the colour is encoded on a bit that can take 2 values (0 and 1). For a black and white raster image, each pixel is encoded by 1 black or white bit.

b) Coding a greyscale image

Greyscale is a range of monochromatic shades from black to white. Consequently, a greyscale image contains only shades of grey and no colour. All that is encoded here is the level light intensity, generally on one byte (256 values). By convention, the value zero represents black (zero light intensity) and the value 255 represents white (maximum light intensity).

c) Coding a colour image

Colour is encoded in three bytes, each byte representing the value of a colour component by an integer from 0 to 255. These three values generally encode the colour in RGB space. The number of different colours that can be represented in this way is 256 x 256 x 256 possibilities, or nearly 16 million colours. As the difference in nuance between two colours that are very close but different in this mode of representation is almost imperceptible For the human eye, it is convenient to assume that this system provides an accurate reproduction of colours, which is why they are referred to as true colours.

II.4. General diagram of a character recognition system [17]

A recognition system takes the form of a set of modules, starting with the acquisition of the characters to be recognised and ending with their actual recognition. In this section we focus on off-line recognition systems, presenting the main stages in a handwriting recognition chain. We will look at the following phases: acquisition (scanning, digitisation), pre-processing, segmentation, feature extraction and, if necessary, classification.

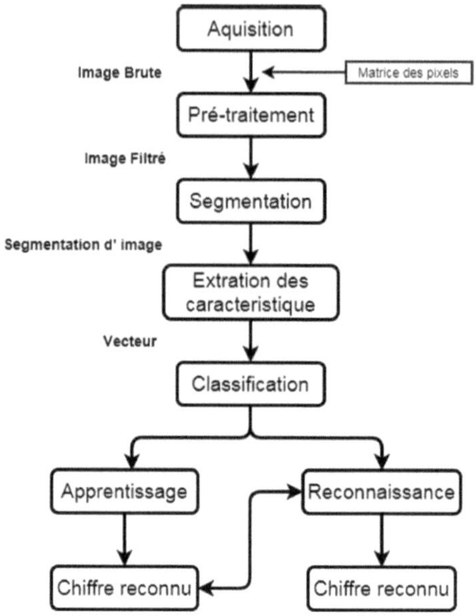

Figure II.2: General diagram a digit recognition system

II.4.1. Image acquisition

This phase consists of capturing the image of a text using physical sensors (scanner, camera, etc.) and converting it into digital quantities suitable for the processing system, with as little degradation as possible. They can also capture images in grey scale (up to 256 levels) or even in colour. The figures are written on paper (cheques or plain paper) and acquired by scanner or camera.

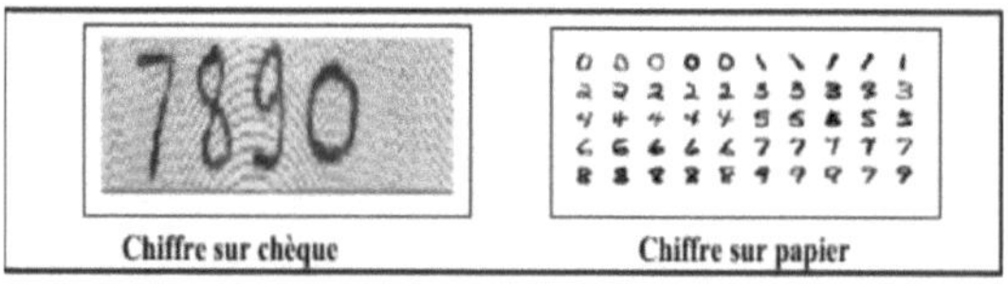

Figure II.3 :Acquired images [17]

There are two types acquisition: offline acquisition and online acquisition. each with its own acquisition tools and corresponding recognition algorithms.

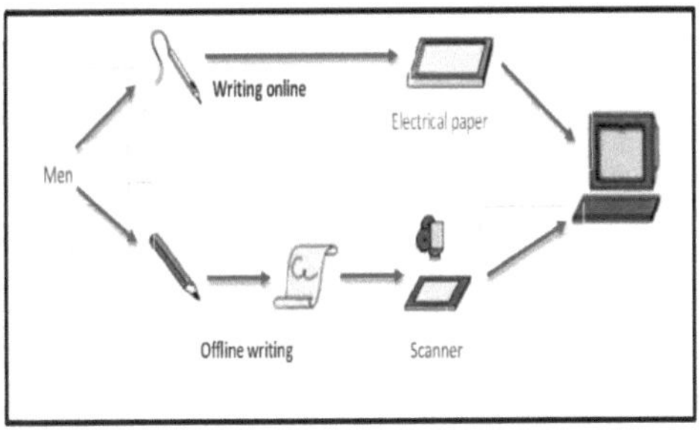

Figure II.4: Human-machine write communication [17]

a) Offline writing acquisition ;

This involves recognising handwritten texts from previously written documents. The image of the written text is digitised using a scanner or line-scan cameras, and the information gathered takes the form of a discrete image made up of a set of pixels. The resolution of the digitised image influences the subsequent stages of an automatic reading system

b) Learning write online ;

The most common acquisition devices are digitising tablets or electronic paper. Sampling the trace provides a series of coordinates describing the trajectory of the pen time. The more advanced tablets also provide access to pen pressure and tilt information.

II.4.2. Pre-treatment

Image pre-processing consists of eliminating the noise due to the acquisition conditions, and retaining only the significant information about the shape represented to facilitate subsequent processing. If the acquisition was carried out in greyscale or colour, binarisation will often be one of these pre-processing operations. The pre-processing operations generally used include: binarisation, noise removal, normalisation and skeletonisation, handwriting rectification, etc.

a) Binarisation of the image

Binarisation is the conversion of a colour image, defined by several levels of grey, into a bitonal image (made up of two values 0 and 1) which allows classification between the background (image of the paper support in white) and the form (lines of engravings and characters in black).

Several techniques have been developed to transform a greyscale or colour image into a binary image. All these techniques are based on the principle of thresholding, as shown in the following equation:

$$I_b(x,y)=\begin{cases}0 \text{ si } In(x,y) < T \\ 1 \text{ si } In(x,y) \geq T\end{cases}$$

$I_n(x, y)$ describes the intensity at "n" levels of grey at each point in the image,$I_b(x, y)$ represents the intensity at two levels and T is the binarisation threshold. If $I_n(x, y)$ is greater than the threshold value, then the image point corresponding to the maximum intensity value (white) is assigned. Otherwise, the point is considered black and is assigned the minimum intensity value. The following figure illustrates the binarisation stage:

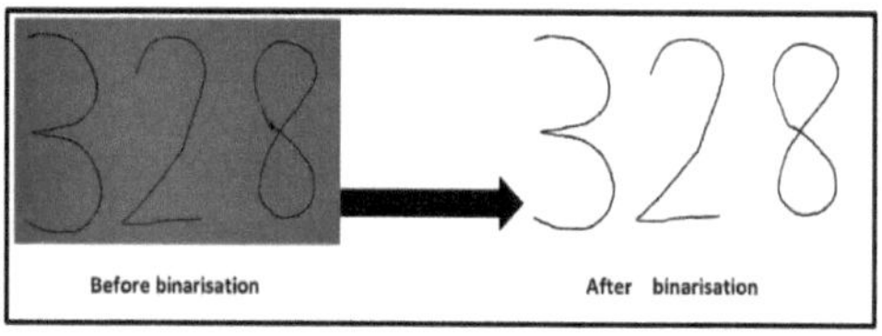

Figure II.5: Example of binarisation [17].

The role of thresholding is to eliminate unwanted points and give a clear image that can be distinguished from the background. According to the binarisation thresholding principle, there are two types of binarisation: global thresholding and adaptive thresholding.

✓ Global thresholding: Global thresholding consists of setting an adjustable threshold that is identical for the entire image. Each pixel in the image is compared with this threshold and takes the value white or black depending on whether it is higher or lower. The classification then depends only on the grey level of the pixel in question.

✓ Adaptive thresholding: a binarisation threshold is calculated for each pixel in the image by depending on its neighbourhood.

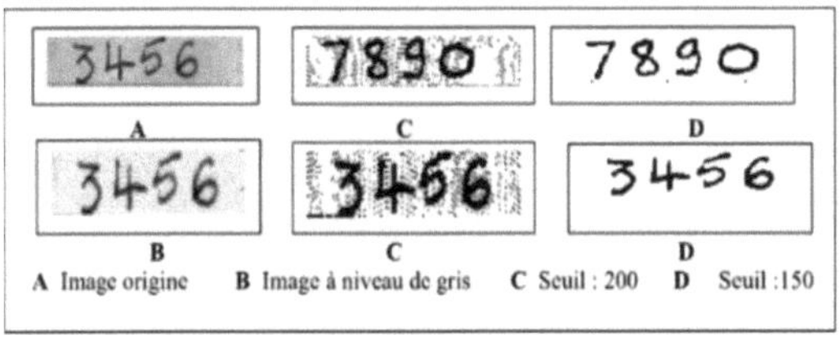

Figure II.6 :Images at different thresholds [17].

The threshold must be calculated carefully, as there is often a risk of losing the information. as the examples show.

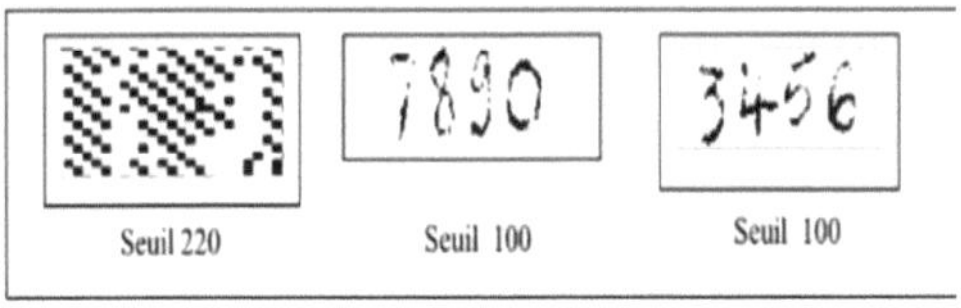

Figure II.7: Different thresholds for a black and white image [17]

b) Noise elimination

The problem of noise is very important but very difficult, particularly when the user is writing on a sheet with a complex background such as coloured paper. A simple technique is to subtract the input image from the image on the coloured paper (there is no writing). However, the two images must be aligned and any writing that crosses the background elements will be removed.

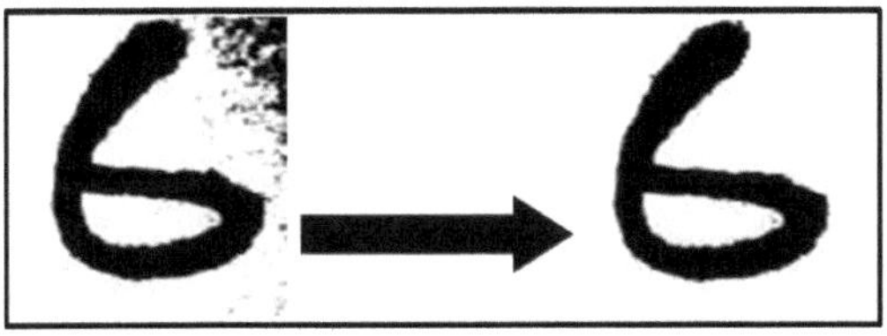

Figure II.8: Example of noise elimination [17].

c) Image normalisation

To facilitate the recognition stage, the segmented digits must be standardised to a fixed size. The main constraint lies in the choice of this size. If it is too small, there a risk of losing information; if it is too large, the recognition stage will operate slowly.

d) Skeletonisation

The aim of this technique is to simplify the character image into a 'line' image that is easier to process, by reducing it to the outline of the character. Skeletonisation algorithms are based on iterative methods. The process is carried out in successive passes to determine whether a particular pixel is essential in order to keep it in the trace or not. The output of this process is a skeleton of a handwritten character.

e) Straightening handwriting

One of the problems encountered in character recognition is the slant of lines of text, which introduces difficulties for segmentation. The slant may come from the input, if the document has been placed at an angle, or it may be intrinsic to the text. In this case, the text needs to be straightened to restore the horizontal line structure of a text image. If α is the angle of inclination, to straighten the image an isometric rotation of angle -α is performed using the following linear transformation:

$x^{r} = x \cos a + y \sin a$

$\{y' = y \cos a + x \sin a$

II.4.3. Segmentation

To simplify the recognition task, segmentation enables the string of handwritten digits to be divided into several entities. This involves dividing the string of digits into several images, each containing an isolated digit.

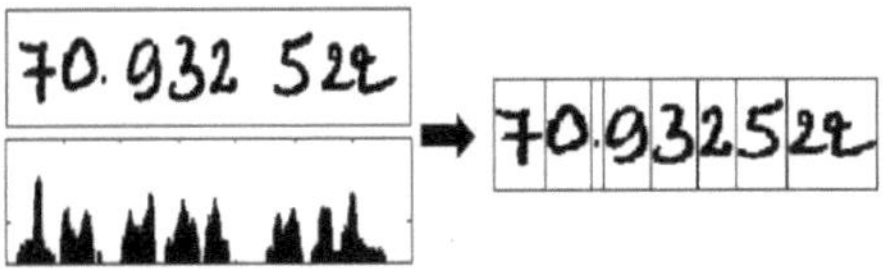

Figure II.9: Segmentation of figures using the vertical projection histogram [17]

In practice, two segmentation stages are necessary. The first stage is primary segmentation, which separates characters according to zero crossings (or by using a predefined threshold) of the vertical projection histogram. At the end of this stage, not all linked, overlapped or partially overlapped digits are segmented. There is also a risk that the fragmented digits will be split in two. For this reason, the second stage, known as secondary segmentation, defines segmentation rules based on an analysis of connection types.

II.4.4. Feature extraction

Feature extraction involves transforming an image (figure, etc.) into a fixed-size feature vector. This transformation involves changing the data representation space from the image plane to an n-dimensional space. The choice of characteristics is critical, and has a clear influence on the result. These features must have the following properties:

✓ Discrimination: enabling good differentiation between the classes of symbols to be recognised.

✓ Limited number of dimensions: the curse of dimensionality must be avoided in order to maintain a limited number of dimensions.

✓ Invariant: features must be invariant to translation, rotation and change of scale, and they must also be independent of distortion and noise.

II.4.5. Classification

Classification involves assigning a given shape to a predefined class. This phase combines two tasks: learning and recognition. In this stage, the features from the previous stage are used to identify a text segment and assign it to a reference model.

a) Learning

In the case of learning, it is a matter of providing the system with a set of shapes which are already known (the class of each of them is known). It is this training set that will enable the recognition system to be adjusted so that it is capable of recognising shapes of unknown classes at a later date.

Learning consists of two different concepts: training and adaptation. Training involves teaching the system how to describe characteristics, while adaptation is used to improve the system's performance by learning from previous experience.

b) Recognition and decision :

The decision is the final recognition stage. Based on the parameter description of the trait, the recognition module looks for the closest reference models available. Recognition can lead to success if the response is unique (a single model matches the description of the shape of the character). It can lead to confusion if the response is multiple (several models match the description). Finally, it can lead to rejection of the shape if no model matches its description. In the first two cases, the decision can be accompanied by a likelihood measure, also known as a score or recognition rate.

II.5. Conclusion

In this chapter we have briefly presented the field of pattern recognition, an important task used in classification, and we have focused more on character recognition, which is the area that interests us most in this work. A general five-stage model has been introduced. This generally reflects the recognition process. It should be noted that there are different ways of approaching this field and that there are no key methods for the automatic processing of a given script. In our work, we use a recognition system based on a convolutional neural network. The following chapter gives a detailed description of this classification method applied to the recognition of handwritten digits.

CHAPTER III

CONVOLUTIONAL NEURAL NETWORKS

III.1. Introduction

Neural networks, which are made up of artificial cellular structures, offer a new approach to the problems of perception, memory, learning and reasoning. They are also proving to be very promising alternatives for circumventing some of the limitations of conventional computers. Thanks to their parallel processing of information and their mechanisms, inspired by nerve cells (neurons), they infer emergent properties that enable us to solve problems that were once described as complex. The aim of this chapter is to present convolutional neural networks (CNNs). To do this, a general presentation of CNNs is required, followed by a detailed look at the different layers, then the choice of parameters and the presentation of different regulation methods. Finally, the advantages of CNNs will be discussed to conclude this chapter.

III.2. General information on CNNs [3]

Convolutional neural networks are specially designed to process input images. They are the most powerful in terms image classification. These networks have two distinct parts. The first part is the convolutional part, which is what makes this type of network so special. This part works like a feature extractor. An image passes through a succession of convolution filters. Usually, a convolution layer is followed by an activation function. Some intermediate filters are there to reduce the resolution of the image by a local maximum operation. This process can be repeated several times. Finally, the convolution maps are concatenated into a vector, called the CNN code. This vector represents the output of the first block and the input of the second.The second part is not characteristic of a CNN, but consists of a fully connected layer. The role of this part is to combine the characteristics of the CNN code to classify the image. The output is a final layer containing as many elements as there classes. The numerical values obtained are generally normalised between 0 and 1, with a sum of 1, for produce a probability distribution over the categories. As with ordinary neural networks, the layer parameters are determined by gradient back propagation. However, in the case of CNNs, these parameters refer in particular to the features of the images.

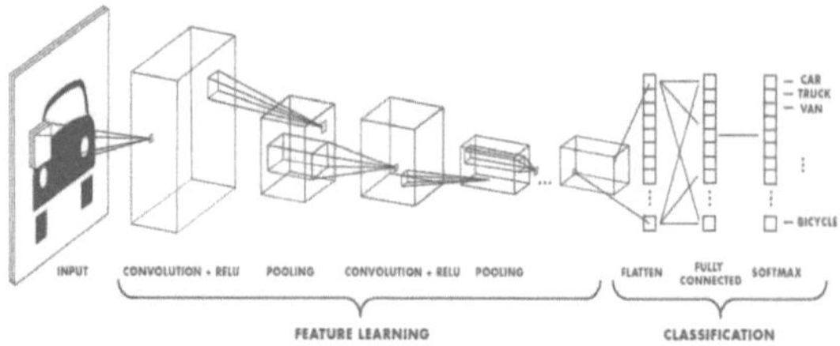

Figure III.1: Standard architecture of a convolutional neural network [Https://medium.com/@RaghavPrabhu/understanding-of-convolutional-neural-network-cnn-deep-learning-99760835f148].

III.3. Different layers a CNN [16]

A CNN architecture consists of a stack of independent processing layers:

✓ The convolution layer, which processes the data from a receiver field.

✓ The pooling layer, which compresses the information by reducing the size of the intermediate image (often by sub-sampling).

✓ The correction layer, often mistakenly called ReLU in reference to the activation function (Linear Rectification Unit).

✓ The "fully connected" layer, which is a perceptron-type layer.

✓ The loss layer (LOSS)

III.3.1. Convolution layer

a) Operating principle

The convolution layer is the key component of CNNs, and is present in at least the first layer. The aim of this layer is to find a set of features in the images received as input. This is where the convolution operation comes in: the principle is to 'drag' a window representing the feature onto the image. In this case, the feature is considered to be a filter. The filters correspond exactly to the features we want to find in the images. The output is a feature map showing the location of the features in the image. In a CNN, the features are not predefined according to a particular formalism as in traditional methods; they are learned during the network training phase. CNNs are therefore capable of determining the discriminating features of an image all by themselves.

b) **Calculation of output dimensions** [8] [3] [24]

Calculating the size of the output associated with a convolution layer requires knowledge of three hyper-parameters.

✓ Step: in the context of a convolution operation, the step or "stride" refers to the step by which the kernel is moved through the image after each operation.

✓ Depth: this is the number of convolution kernels or filters.

✓ Zero padding: it is common to use a margin of zeros around the input. Zero padding is a technique that consists of adding P zeros to each side of the input borders.

Let I be the side associated with the input, F the size of the core, P the thickness of the zero margin and s the amplitude of the step used; the dimension O of the output is then given by :

$$O = \frac{I - F + 2P}{S} + 1$$

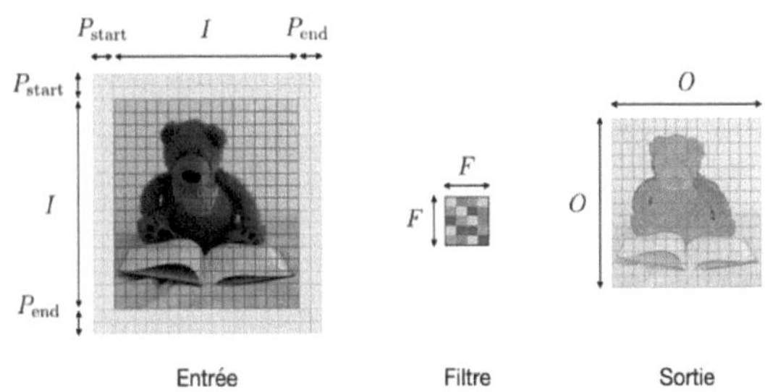

Figure III.2 : Illustration of the size of a convolution layer output [Https://stanford.edu/~shervine/l/en/teaching/cs-230/pense-bete-reseaux-neurones-convolutionnels].

$$O = \frac{I + F + P_{start} + P_{end}}{S}$$

III.3.2. Pooling layer

a) Operating principle [8]

The pooling layer is often placed between two convolution layers. It applies a pooling operation, which is a sub-sampling operation. It consists of reducing the size of images, while preserving their important characteristics. To do this, the image is divided into regular cells of size 2 × 2 pixels which do not overlap, or of size 3 × 3 pixels, spaced apart by a step of 2 pixels (which therefore overlap). pooling operation is then applied. The outputs obtained are the same number as the inputs but smaller in size. The pooling layer reduces the number of parameters and calculations in the network. This improves the efficiency of the network and prevents overlearning.

b) The pooling operation [20] [24]

The idea behind the pooling operation is to remove a certain amount of information from the same neighbourhood for the input. The operation is performed on each of the thicknesses linked to the depth of the input. Generally, max or average pooling is used, where the maximum and average values are taken respectively.

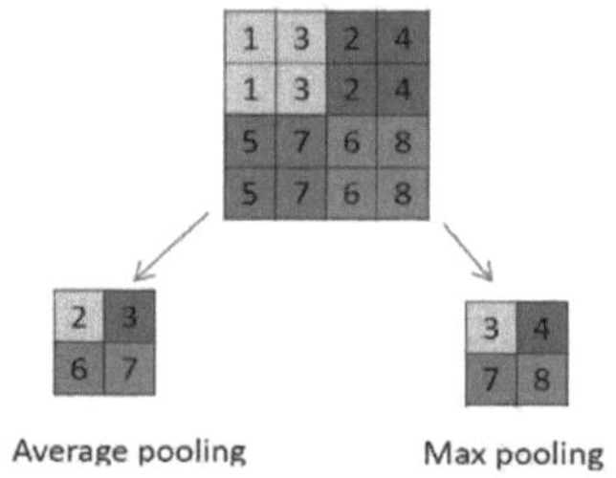

Figure III.3: Example of calculation of Max pooling and Average pooling [Https://en.quora.com/Quest-que-que-le-pooling-maximum-dans-les-r%C3%A9seaux-de-neurones-].convolutional]

average pooling: each box corresponds to the average of the input square of the same For example, in the case of the yellow square, we have :

$$\frac{1+3+3+1}{4} = 2$$

For max pooling: each box corresponds to the maximum value the input square of the same colour, e.g. for the blue box :

$$\max(5,7,5,7) = 7$$

III.3.3. Rectified Linear Units layer [24]

The ReLU or Rectified Linear Units function is applied after the convolution function and leaves the dimensions unchanged. It is a non-linear real function defined by :

$$ReLU(x) = \max(0, x)$$

The ReLU correction therefore replaces all negative input values with zeros. It acts as an activation function and is designed to introduce non-linear complexities into the network.

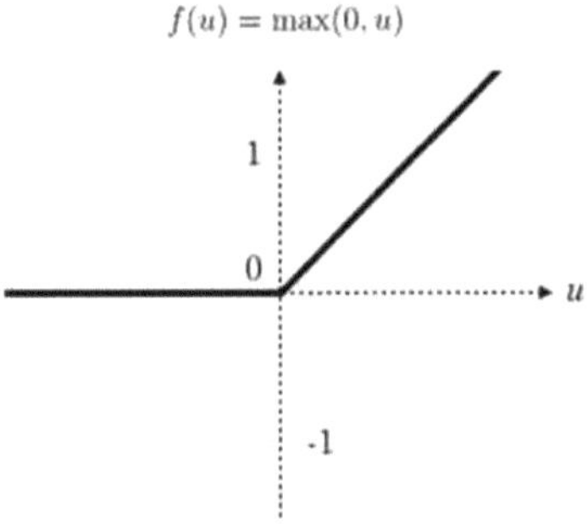

Figure III.4 : Rectified Linear Units function

III.3.4. Fully connected layer [3][8]

The fully-connected layer is always the last layer of a neural network. This layer is therefore not characteristic of a CNN. It is applied to a previously flattened input where each input is connected to all the neurons and produces a new vector at the output.The last layer classifies the input image into several classes and returns a vector whose size is equal to the number of classes in the problem. Each element of the vector indicates the probability of the input image belonging to a certain class.To calculate the probabilities, the fully connected layer multiplies each input element by a weight, adds them together and then applies an activation function (here we use the soft max function if the number of classes is$N > 2$ or logistic sigmoid if

$N = 2$). The weights are learned during the training phase, by back propagation of the gradient.The fully connected layer looks for links between the position of features in the image and a class. The input table corresponds to an activation map for a given feature: high values indicate the location of this feature in the image. If the location of a feature at a certain point in the image is characteristic of a certain class, then the corresponding value in the table is given significant weight.

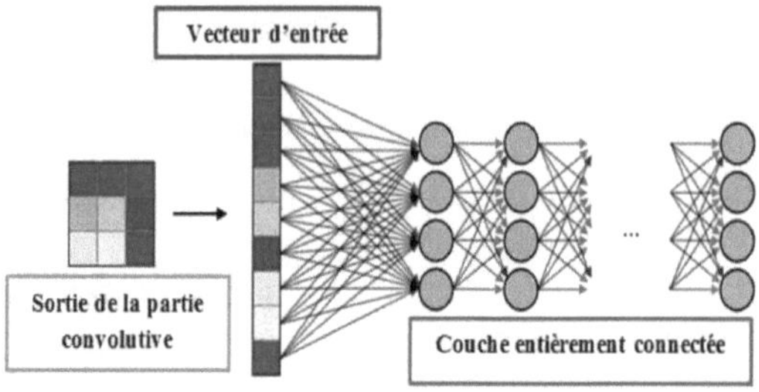

Figure III.5 : Demonstration of a fully connected layer [Https://stanford.edu/~shervine/l/en/teaching/cs-230/pense-bete-reseaux-neurones-convolutionnels].

III.3.5. Loss layer (LOSS)

It is normally the last layer in the network. Various loss functions adapted different tasks can be used here. The Softmax function is used on the output classes.

III.4. Choice of parameters [14]

CNNs use more hyper-parameters than a standard multilayer network. Even if the usual rules for learning rates and regularisation constants still apply, the notions of number of filters, their shape and the form of max pooling need to be taken into account.

III.4.1. Number of filters

The size of intermediate images decreases with the depth of processing, with layers closer to the input tending to have fewer filters while layers closer to the output may have more. To equalise the calculation at each layer, the product of the number of features and the number of pixels processed is generally chosen to be approximately constant across the layers.To preserve the input information, the number of intermediate outputs (number of intermediate images, multiplied by the number of pixel positions) should be maintained to grow (in the broadest sense) from one layer to the next. The number of intermediate images directly controls the power of the system, depends on the number of examples available and the complexity of the processing.

III.4.2. Filter shape

Filter shapes vary widely in the literature. They are generally chosen according to the dataset. The best results on MNIST images (28x28) are usually in the range of 5x5 on the first layer, whereas natural image datasets (often with hundreds of pixels in each dimension) tend to use larger first layer filters of 12x12 or even 15x15. The challenge is therefore to findthe right level of granularity to create abstractions at the appropriate scale for each case.

III.4.3. Form of max pooling

Typical values are 2x2. Very large input volumes may justify 4x4 pooling in the first layers. However, choosing larger shapes will considerably reduce the size of the signal, and may result in the loss of too much information.

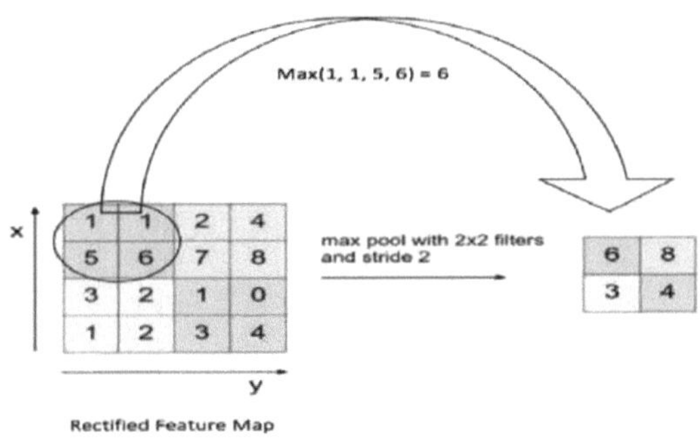

Figure III.6 : Example of max pooling (2×2) [Https://vinova.sg/2019/10/30/an-intuitive-explanation-of-convolutional-neural-networks-the-data-science-blog/]

III.5. Regularisation method [21]

To deal with problems of overlearning, there are regularisation methods to be used:

✓ Empirical methods

✓ Explicit methods

III.5.1. Empirical methods

a) Dropout

The FC (Fully Connected) layers take up most of the CNN's memory. In fact, the FC concept creates an exponential memory problem called over-connection (leading to over-learning), which slows down information processing. To avoid this, the dropout method is used to randomly switch off neurons with a probability of neurons, often one neuron in two, as well as the peripheral neurons. With fewer neurons, the network is more reactive and can therefore learn more quickly. At the end of the learning session, the switched-off neurons are switched back on with their original weights. The closer the FC layer is to the source image, the fewer neurons will be switched off.

The aim is to switch the neurons off and on again randomly, as part of successive training sessions. Once the training series is complete, all the neurons are switched back on and the network is used as usual. This technique not only showed a gain in learning speed, but by disconnecting the neurons we also limited marginal effects, making the network more robust and better able to generalise the concepts learned.

b) DropConnect

DropConnect is an evolution of dropout, in which we no longer switch off a neuron, but a connection (the equivalent of the synapse), always at random. The results are similar (speed, ability to generalise learning), but there is a difference in the evolution of connection weights. An FC layer with a DropConnect can be likened to a diffuse connection layer.

c) Stochastic pooling

Stochastic pooling uses the same principle as Max-pooling, but the selected output is taken at random, according to a multinomial distribution defined as a function of the activity of the zone addressed by the pool. In practice, this system is similar to Max-pooling with a large number of similar images, which vary only through localised distortions.

III.5.2. Explicit methods

a) Network size

The simplest way to limit overlearning is to limit the number of layers in the network and free up the free parameters (connections) in the network. This directly reduces the power and predictive potential of the network.

b) Weight loss

The concept is to consider the weight vector of a neuron, the list of weights associated with the incoming signals, and to add to it an error vector proportional to the sum of the weights or the square of the weights. This error vector can then be multiplied by a proportionality coefficient, which can be increased to further penalise vectors with high weights.

III.6. Model validation

Validation also applies to any other supervised learning method. It involves studying the performance of the model we have built, and here we are trying to estimate the classification errors of our model, i.e. the probability that it correctly predicts the output class of a datum. Intuitively, we can see that this error corresponds to the probability that the classifier will fail to predict the class of a new datum. We list a few performance indicators for a predictive model.

✓ **Confusion matrix [28]**

The confusion matrix shows the quality of a model. Each of its columns represents the number of occurrences of a class predicted by the classifier, while each of its rows represents the number of occurrences of a target class (desired class or expected output class). The data considered may come from the training set or from a set of data reserved for testing.

The results are divided into 4 categories:

- True Positive (TP): the prediction and the actual value are positive.
- True Negative (TN): the prediction and the actual value are negative.
- False Positive (FP): the prediction is positive whereas the actual value is negative.
- False Negative (FN): the prediction is negative whereas the actual value is positive.

Table III.1: Confusion matrix

		Classe predite	
		Positive	Négative
Classe actuelle	Positive	Vraie positive (VP)	Faux négative (FN) Type d'erreur II
	Négative	Faux positive (FP) Type d'erreur I	Vraie négative (VN)

Of course, rows and columns can be added to this matrix in more complex cases. We can calculate the various indicators summarising the confusion matrix. If we want to account for the quality of the prediction on the class to be predicted, we define :

• Accuracy: proportion of items well classified for a given class:

$$Précision = \frac{VP}{VP+FP}$$

• Reminder: proportion well-ranked items in relation to the number items in the class to predict :

$$Rappel = \frac{VP}{VP+FN}$$

• F-measure: measurement of the trade-off between precision and recall : 2 x (precision x recall)

$$F\_mesure = \frac{2 \times (précision \times rappel)}{précision + rappel}$$

III.7. Advantages of CNNs [14]

A major advantage of convolutional networks is the use of a single weight associated with the signals entering all the neurons in a single convolution kernel. This method reduces the memory footprint, improves performance and enables translation-invariant processing. This is the main advantage of CNN over MLP, which considers each neuron independent and therefore assigns a different weight to each incoming signal. Compared to other classification algorithms, convolutional neural networks use relatively little pre-processing. This means that the network is responsible for evolving its own filters on its own (unsupervised learning), which is not the case with other more traditional algorithms. The absence of initial parameterisation and human intervention is a major advantage of CNNs.

III.8. Conclusion

In this chapter, we presented convolutional neural networks. These networks are capable of extracting features from input images and classifying these features. They are based on the notion of receptive fields, and also implement the idea of weight sharing, which makes it possible to reduce the number of free parameters in the architecture.This sharing of weights also makes it possible to reduce computing times and the memory space required, as well as improving the network's generalisation capabilities. The next chapter will be devoted to the model design and then to interpreting the results obtained in the learning and testing phase.

CHAPTER IV

IMPLEMENTATION AND INTERPRETATION OF RESULTS

IV.1. Presentation of the case

We have chosen the banking sector as the application domain for our work, where our aim is to build a system for recognising the amount written on a bank cheque, by means of an automatic classifier that will recognise the characters making up the amount one after the other (isolation).Automatic processing of bank cheques requires prior segmentation of the various information zones on the cheque. Among these zones, one contains the sequence of handwritten digits that translate the amount to be withdrawn. This part is of particular interest to us in this work.Cheques have a particular document structure. A study of the physical and logical structure is necessary for our segmentation method. It gives the preliminary position of each component of the cheque. The physical structure indicates the nature of the content of each component and the logical structure presents the meaning of the content of the zone.

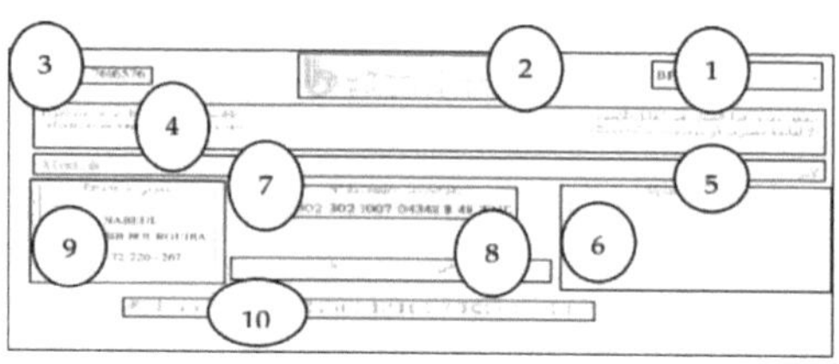

Figure IV.1: Physical and logical structure of the cheque [27].

Table IV.1: Physical content and meaning

<table>
<tr><th>Zone number</th><th>Physical interpretation</th><th colspan="4">Logical interpretation</th></tr>
<tr><td>1</td><td>Handwritten digits and printed script</td><td colspan="4">The numerical amount</td></tr>
<tr><td>2</td><td>Printed text
and image</td><td colspan="4">The name and acronym of the bank</td></tr>
<tr><td>3</td><td>Writing and digits
Printed matter</td><td colspan="4">The cheque number</td></tr>
<tr><td>4</td><td>Printed text
and handwritten</td><td colspan="4">The amount in words</td></tr>
<tr><td>5</td><td>Printed text
and handwritten</td><td colspan="4">The name of the receiver</td></tr>
<tr><td>6</td><td>Image</td><td>Thewriter's number</td><td>from</td><td>account</td><td>from</td></tr>
<tr><td>7</td><td>Writing and digits
Printed matter</td><td>Thewriter's number</td><td>from</td><td>account</td><td>from</td></tr>
<tr><td>8</td><td>Writing and digits
Printed matter</td><td colspan="4">The address and the number of bank telephone</td></tr>
<tr><td>9</td><td>Writing and digits
Printed matter</td><td colspan="4">The address andthe number of bank telephone</td></tr>
<tr><td>10</td><td>Printed digits</td><td colspan="4">The cheque number, bank code and account number of the writer</td></tr>
</table>

For automatic recognition of the amount, an extraction step is required. We apply a logical AND between the original image and the constructed mask

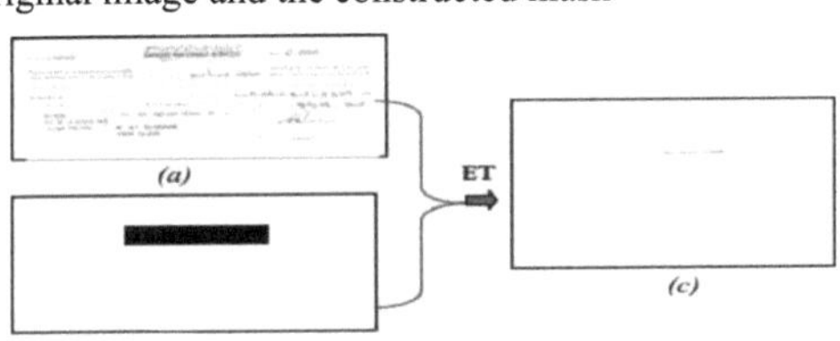

Figure IV.2 :(a) Original image, (b) Mask of the upright area, (c) Extraction area [27].

There are two modules for the recognition system: the first module consists of recognising the amount written on the cheque and identifying the owner of the cheque by means of the account number still written on the cheque, after which the system will segment each sequence of digits appearing in the two zones in order to obtain a sequence of isolated digits. After this stage comes the object of our work, which is to recognise each digit isolated from the previous sequences using a convolutional neural network.

IV.2. Tools presentation

IV.2.1. Google colab [30]

The experiments and tests were carried out on Google Colaboratory or Colab, a simple and free Google tool for learning about Deep Learning or collaborating with your colleagues on data science projects. Colab allows :

✓ Improve coding skills in the Python programming language.

✓ Develop Deep Learning applications using popular Python libraries such as Keras, TensorFlow, PyTorch and OpenCV.

✓ Use a development environment (Jupyter Notebook) that requires no configuration.

But the feature that sets Colab apart from other services is access to a GPU graphics processor, completely free of charge!

IV.2.2. Python [31]

Python is a high-level interpreted (there is no compilation stage), object-oriented programming language with dynamic semantics. It is widely used by a large community of developers and programmers. Python is a simple language that is easy to learn and reduces the cost of code maintenance. Python libraries (packages) encourage modularity and code reusability. Python and its libraries are available (source or binaries) free of charge for most platforms and can be redistributed free of charge.

IV.2.3. Tensorflow

TensorFlow is a programming framework for numerical computation that was made Open Source by Google in November 2015. Since its release, TensorFlow has gone from strength to strength, rapidly becoming one of the most widely used frameworks for Deep Learning and neural networks. Its name was inspired in particular by the fact that current operations on neural networks are mainly carried out via multidimensional data tables, known as Tensors. A two-dimensional Tensor is the equivalent of a matrix. Today, Google's main products are based on TensorFlow: Gmail, Google Photos and voice recognition.

IV.2.4. Keras

Keras is a high-level neural network API written in Python and capable of running on TensorFlow or Theano. The Keras library is used to interact with algorithms for deep neural networks and machine learning , in particular Tensorflow and Theano. It is designed to enable rapid experimentation with deep neural networks, and focuses on its usability, modularity and extension capabilities.

IV.2.5. Scikit-learn

Scikit-learn is certainly the library the library the most popular library for automatic learning in Python. contains all the models that we have implemented and many more besides. In real life, you will never build a decision tree from scratch: you will delegate all the heavy lifting to scikit-learn. Likewise, you'll never write an optimisation algorithm by hand: you'll call scikit-learn to find an efficient algorithm straight away. The documentation for this library contains many examples of what it can do (and more generally of what machine learning can do).

IV.2.6. Numpy [32]

This is a library for manipulating matrices or multidimensional arrays and the mathematical functions that operate on these arrays. It has arrays that are more powerful than our list vectors, matrices that are more powerful than our list matrices and offers many ready-to-use numerical functions. NumPy is a basic block that serves as a foundation for many libraries, which makes it particularly interesting.

IV.2.7. Matplotlib [33]

This is a library in the Python programming language for plotting and displaying data in graphical form. It can be combined with the NumPy and SciPy scientific computing libraries. Matplotlib is freely distributed.

IV.2.8. Seaborn [34]

It is a library that is added to Matplotlib, replaces certain default settings and functions, and adds new functions. Seaborn corrects Matplotlib's shortcomings.

IV.3. MNIST database [35]

The MNIST database (Modified or Mixed National Institute of Standards and Technology) is a database of handwritten numbers. It is a dataset that is widely used in machine learning. The database contains 70,000 images from a previous database, simply called NIST. The images are black and white, standardised and centred at 28 pixels per side.For our first experiments, we are going to use the MNIST database, which contains descriptions of handwritten digits in 28 × 28 format, i.e. 784 pixels, and the associated labels. The database contains a total of 70,000 examples, i.e. 7,000 examples of each digit.First we load the database, then we examine one of the examples it contains. We select 60,000 examples for learning and 10,000 for testing (the MNIST database is organised in this way).For future tests, it is important to ensure that the examples are randomly distributed in the training database so that each draw from a subset contains approximately the same proportion of each digit.

Figure IV.3: Sample of figures from the MNIST database [Https://intelligence-artificielle.agency/mnist-lecture-de-la-base/].

IV.4. Model architecture

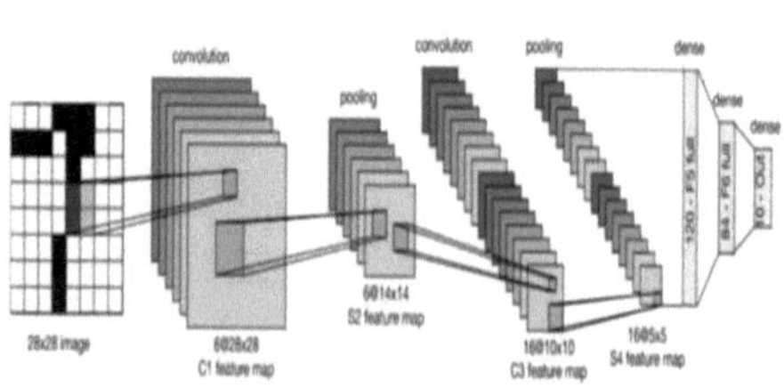

Figure IV.4: Architecture of the model [Https://medium.com/mlearning-ai/lenet-and-mnist-handwritten-digit-classification-354f5646c590]

The architecture of the model we are presenting is made up of two layers of convolution, two layers of maxpooling and three layers of fully connected. The input image is 28*28 in size, and first passes through the first convolution layer. This layer is made up of 32 filters of size 3*3, each of our convolution layers is followed by a ReLU activation function, this function forces the neurons to return positive values, after this convolution 32 feature maps of size 28*28 will be created, then we apply Maxpooling to reduce the size of the image and the amount of parameters and calculation. At the end of this layer, we will have 32 feature maps of size 14*14.The 32 feature maps obtained previously are given as input to the second convolution layer, which is made up of 64 filters. A ReLU activation is applied to the convolution layer, then Maxpooling is applied to reduce the size of the image. At the output of this layer, we will have 64 feature maps of size 6*6. After these layers comes the dropout, which randomly sets the output of certain neurons to zero. The feature vector resulting from the convolutions has a dimension of 2304 pixels. We then use a neural network made up of three fully connected layers. The first layer has 120 neurons where the activation function used is the ReLu, the second layer has 84 neurons and finally the last layer has 10 neurons where the activation function is a softmax which is used to calculate the probability distribution of the 10 classes.

Table IV.2: Model configuration

Model: "sequential"

Layer (type)	Output Shape	Param #
conv2d (Conv2D)	(None, 28, 28, 32)	320
max_pooling2d (MaxPooling2D)	(None, 14, 14, 32)	0
conv2d_1 (Conv2D)	(None, 12, 12, 64)	18496
max_pooling2d_1 (MaxPooling2D)	(None, 6, 6, 64)	0
dropout (Dropout)	(None, 6, 6, 64)	0
flatten (Flatten)	(None, 2304)	0
dense (Dense)	(None, 84)	193620
dropout_1 (Dropout)	(None, 84)	0
dense_1 (Dense)	(None, 120)	10200
dropout_2 (Dropout)	(None, 120)	0
dense_2 (Dense)	(None, 10)	1210

Total params: 223,846
Trainable params: 223,846
Non-trainable params: 0

IV.5. Implementing the model

IV.5.1. Importing libraries

This stage consists of importing the libraries that will facilitate the construction of the model

```
[ ] import tensorflow as tf
    import keras
    import matplotlib.pyplot as plt
    import random
    import numpy as np
    import seaborn as sn
    from tensorflow.keras.models import Sequential
    from tensorflow.keras.layers import Dense, Conv2D, Dropout, Flatten, MaxPooling2D
    from tensorflow.keras.models import Sequential
    from tensorflow.keras.layers import Dense, Conv2D, Dropout, Flatten, MaxPooling2D
```

Figure IV.5 : Importing libraries

IV.5.2. Importing the dataset

This stage involves importing the data that will be used training and testing.

```
[ ] mnist = tf.keras.datasets.mnist
    (x_train, y_train),(x_test,y_test) = mnist.load_data()

    Downloading data from https://storage.googleapis.com/tensorflow/tf-keras-datasets/mnist.npz
    11493376/11490434 [==============================] - 0s 0us/step
    11501568/11490434 [==============================] - 0s 0us/step
```

Figure IV.6 : Importing data

IV.5.3. Cutting

This step consists of dividing all the data in the MNIST database into trains and tests: 60,000 sample images training and 10,000 for testing

```
[ ]
    print('Number of images in x_train', x_train.shape[0])
    print('Nomber of images in x_test', x_test.shape[0])

    Number of images in x_train 60000
    Nomber of images in x_test 10000
```

Figure IV.7: Data breakdown

IV.5.4. Data visualisation

At this stage we display the dataset data

```
fig = plt.figure()
for i in range(9):
  plt.subplot(3,3,i+1)
  plt.tight_layout()
  plt.imshow(x_train[i], cmap='gray', interpolation='none')
  plt.title("Digit: {}".format(y_train[i]))
  plt.xticks([])
  plt.yticks([])
fig
```

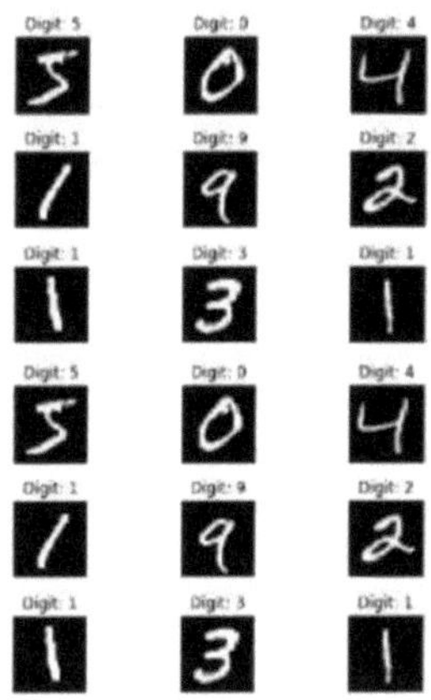

Figure IV.8: Data display

IV.5.5. Resize

This step involves assigning a new size to each image. In this context, the size to be assigned to the images will be the same regardless of the original size of the image to be recognised. We will crop all the images into a 28x28 pixel box.

```
x_train = x_train.reshape(x_train.shape[0], 28, 28, 1)
x_test = x_test.reshape(x_test.shape[0], 28, 28, 1)
input_shape = (28, 28, 1)
x_train = x_train.astype('float32')
x_test = x_test.astype('float32')
x_train /= 255
x_test /= 255
print('x_train shape:', x_train.shape)
print('x_test shape:', x_test.shape)

x_train shape: (60000, 28, 28, 1)
x_test shape: (10000, 28, 28, 1)
```

Figure IV.9:Resizing

IV.5.6. Building the model

This stage is devoted to building the model

```
[ ] model = Sequential()
    model.add(Conv2D(32, kernel_size=(3,3),padding = 'same' ,activation='relu', input_shape= (28,28,1)))
    model.add(MaxPooling2D(pool_size=(2, 2)))
    model.add(Conv2D(64, (3, 3), activation='relu'))
    model.add(MaxPooling2D(pool_size=(2, 2)))
    model.add(Dropout(0.25))
    model.add(Flatten())
    model.add(Dense(64, activation='relu'))
    model.add(Dropout(0.5))
    model.add(Dense(128, activation='relu'))
    model.add(Dropout(0.5))
    model.add(Dense(10, activation='softmax'))
    model.summary()
```

Figure IV.10 :Model scripts

IV.5.7. Model training

We trained our model over 10 epochs obtained the following results: 98.84 % accuracy and 4.42% loss.

```
[ ] model.compile(optimizer='adam',loss='sparse_categorical_crossentropy', metrics=['accuracy'])
    hist=model.fit(x_train, y_train,epochs =10,batch_size = 10,shuffle = True,validation_split = 0.2)

    Epoch 1/10
    4800/4800 [==============================] - 87s 18ms/step - loss: 0.3469 - accuracy: 0.8923 - val_loss: 0.0611 - val_accuracy: 0.9826
    Epoch 2/10
    4800/4800 [==============================] - 85s 18ms/step - loss: 0.1428 - accuracy: 0.9600 - val_loss: 0.0499 - val_accuracy: 0.9869
    Epoch 3/10
    4800/4800 [==============================] - 90s 19ms/step - loss: 0.1105 - accuracy: 0.9679 - val_loss: 0.0489 - val_accuracy: 0.9874
    Epoch 4/10
    4800/4800 [==============================] - 101s 21ms/step - loss: 0.1024 - accuracy: 0.9718 - val_loss: 0.0418 - val_accuracy: 0.9890
    Epoch 5/10
    4800/4800 [==============================] - 89s 19ms/step - loss: 0.0947 - accuracy: 0.9747 - val_loss: 0.0453 - val_accuracy: 0.9891
    Epoch 6/10
    4800/4800 [==============================] - 89s 19ms/step - loss: 0.0883 - accuracy: 0.9767 - val_loss: 0.0401 - val_accuracy: 0.9902
    Epoch 7/10
    4800/4800 [==============================] - 103s 21ms/step - loss: 0.0850 - accuracy: 0.9777 - val_loss: 0.0403 - val_accuracy: 0.9899
    Epoch 8/10
    4800/4800 [==============================] - 94s 20ms/step - loss: 0.0773 - accuracy: 0.9784 - val_loss: 0.0380 - val_accuracy: 0.9903
    Epoch 9/10
    4800/4800 [==============================] - 86s 18ms/step - loss: 0.0737 - accuracy: 0.9808 - val_loss: 0.0432 - val_accuracy: 0.9889
    Epoch 10/10
    4800/4800 [==============================] - 87s 18ms/step - loss: 0.0703 - accuracy: 0.9814 - val_loss: 0.0442 - val_accuracy: 0.9884
```

Figure IV.11: Model training

IV.5.8. Model test

After testing our model, it predicts with an accuracy rate of 99.03% and a rate of error of 3.72%.

```
[ ]
    final_loss, final_acc = model.evaluate(x_test, y_test)
    print("final loss: {0:.4f}, final accuracy: {1:.4f}".format(final_loss, final_acc))

    313/313 [==============================] - 4s 14ms/step - loss: 0.0372 - accuracy: 0.9903
    final loss: 0.0372, final accuracy: 0.9903
```

Figure IV.12: Evaluation

IV.5.9. Evaluation of the model

a) The CNN confusion matrix

The confusion matrix measures the quality of a classification system. Each row corresponds to a real class, and each column to an estimated class. One of the advantages of the confusion matrix is that it quickly shows whether a classification system manages to classify correctly.

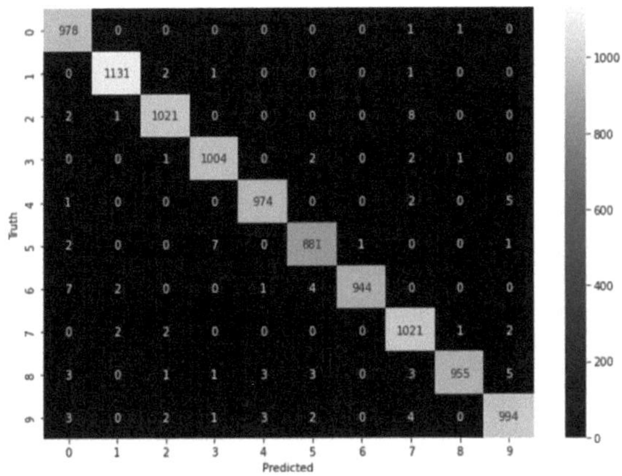

Figure IV.13: Confusion matrix

The confusion matrix can be interpreted as follows:

- ✓ The accuracy of (0)= 978 = 98% chance of correctly predicting 0996
- ✓ The accuracy of (1)= 1131 = 99% chance of correctly predicting 11136
- ✓ The accuracy of (2)= 1021 = 99% chance of correctly predicting 21029
- ✓ The accuracy of (3)= 1004 = 99% chance of correctly predicting 31014
- ✓ The precision of (4)= 974 981
- ✓ The precision of (5)= 881 890
- ✓ The precision of (6)= 944 945

= 99% chance of correctly predicting 4

= 98% chance of correctly predicting 5

= 99% chance of correctly predicting 6

✓ The accuracy of (7)= 1021 = 97% chance of correctly predicting 71042

✓ The precision of (8)= 955 958

✓ The accuracy of (9)= 994 1007

= 99% chance of correctly predicting 8

= 98% chance of correctly predicting 9

b) Precision curve

The curves allow us to ensure that the model is learning correctly. It is important to ensure that the accuracy curve rises with each run (epoch). Ideally, the curve for the validation data should remain close to the curve for the training data (otherwise we need to check whether the model is overlearning or underlearning). According to our results, the blue curve represents the accuracy of our model on the training data, while the red curve gives the accuracy on the test data.

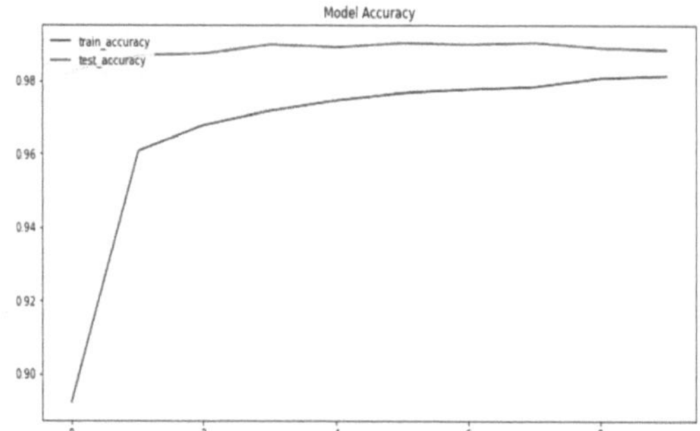

Figure IV.14:Accuracy curve

According to the figure, the accuracy of learning and testing increases with the number of epochs, reflecting the fact that the model learns more information with each epoch. If the accuracy decreases, then we will need more information to make our model learn, so we need to increase the number of epochs.

c) **Loss curve**

The blue curve represents the loss of our model on the training data, while the red curve gives the loss on the test data. The following figure shows the decrease in training and test error with the number of epochs.

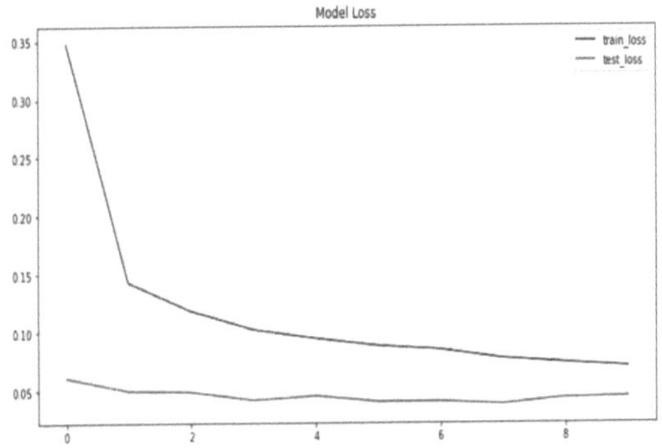

Figure IV.15:Loss curve

IV.5.10. Prediction

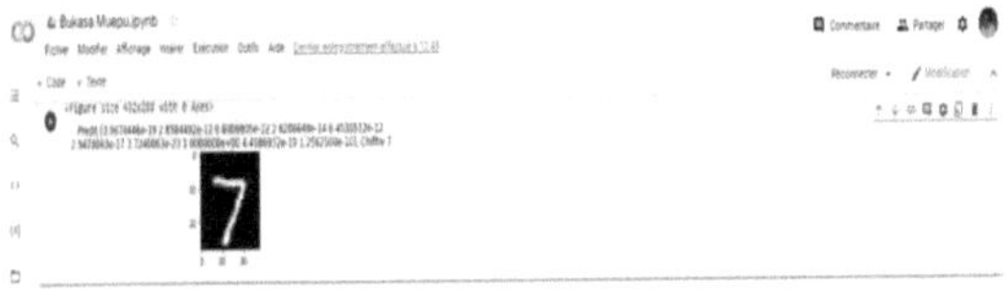

Figure IV.16: Prediction

IV.5.11. Interpretation of results

Table IV.3: Results

	Architecture Used			Number period	Clarification of the learning base	Accuracy of the test base	Error	Time performance
	Convolution layer	Pooling layer	Fully connected					
Model	02	02	03	10	98,84%	99,03%	3,72 %	793 seconds

The table shows the architecture used in the model and the number of epochs. The results obtained are expressed in terms of learning accuracy, test accuracy, error and finally execution time. The execution time is too short. This requires the use of a GPU. The model we have built gives a better result. It predicts with an accuracy rate of 99.03% and an error rate of 3.72%. The number of epochs and convolution layers combined with the execution time reflect these good results. In general, a large and deep convolutional neural network gives good results, but the performance of our network degrades if a convolutional layer is removed.

IV.6. Conclusion

In this chapter we have described the tools used experiment with our model using the convolutional neural network. Based on the adapted indicators, we have seen from the results obtained that learning a model consists of minimising the cost function, which is a parameter that indicates at what level the predicted class is close to the actual class. In our study, we found that the deeper the network, i.e. the more layers are added, the greater the accuracy and the longer the training time. We then evaluated the performance of the model constructed, which proved to be highly effective in terms of its accuracy (99.03%), which is close to perfection.

CONCLUSION

All in all, it has to be said that recognising handwritten numbers is still a major challenge. Despite intensive efforts and work in this area, the challenge remains to improve scores for better results. The aim this work was build, train and optimise a model based on a convolutional neural network, capable of recognising handwritten numbers written on a cheque.To achieve this objective, we used the descriptive method, which enabled us to describe the character recognition process, and the experimental method, which enabled us to experiment with digit recognition using a dataset.We used convolution neural networks to build our model, as they are widely used for image analysis and classification because they can extract features from an image. We tested the model with the MNIST dataset, which contains 70,000 images. We evaluated our model with precision curves, loss curves and the confusion matrix.To implement our model, we used the Python language, which is now indispensable for Machine Learning and Deep Learning applications, as well as a number of libraries, including Scikit-learn, Tensorflow, Keras, Matplotlib, Numpy and Seaborn.At the end of the experiment, the model offers an accuracy of 99%, which is close to perfection. In view of this result, we declare that we have achieved our objective and have confirmed our hypotheses.Admittedly, the physical structure of a bank cheque is very complex, and it contains a great deal of information. Scientists are faced with the difficulty of extracting the different zones in isolation. These difficulties include acquisition, zone extraction and zone segmentation.This work has led us to develop some very interesting perspectives that are line with our research. We want to develop a model for automatic recognition of handwriting, applied to the literal amounts of cheques.

BIBLIOGRAPHY

I. Publications

1. A. conuejols and y. kodratoff, **Apprentissage artificiel : Concepts et algorithmes**, 2003.
2. Chloé-Agathe Azencott, **Introduction to machine learning**, 2018
3. A. Amidi, S. Amidi, **Convolutional neural networks**, 2019.
4. J. Damerji**, Digital image**, 2018.
5. J.M.S. Prewitt, **Object enhancement and extraction**, 1970.
6. L. Likforman-Sulem and E.B. Smith, **Pattern recognition: theory and practice,** 2013.
7. M. J. Vieille**, k-means, how it works**, 2016.
8. P. Monasse, K. Nadjahi, Classify **and segment visual data**, 2019.
9. Yann Le Cun on **predictive learning**, 2016.
10. Y. LeCun, **Les Enjeux de la Recherche en Intelligence Artificielle**, 2016.

II. Course notes

11. Mokhtar Taffar, **Introduction to machine learning**, 2014
12. KAFUNDA KATALAY P, **Intelligence artificiel approfondi**, deuxième licence génie Informatique, University of Mbuji-Mayi, 2021. Unpublished.
13. M. A. Rakotomalala, **Digital Image Processing**, Course M1- TCO, Ment. TCO. - E.S.P.A., A.U.: 2016-2017.II.9

III. Memoirs and articles

14. Boughaba Mohammed et Al, **Deep Learning for the management of the**Content-based image classification and retrieval,2017.
15. C. Imane, K. Ahlam**, La Classification Des Feuilles de Vigne à Base de Descripteur Histogramme de Gradient Orienté,** 2013

16. D.Andriamiandrasoa ianjafitia, **Object detection system based on deep learning in a smart shop,** 2019

17. GUEDIRI Taoufik et al, **Handwritten digit recognition based on support vector machines,** 2016-2017.

18. L.Michel, **L'apprentissage automatique basé sur les réseaux de neurones à convolution for handwritten cipher recognition** ,2016

19. L. Leyrit, **Recognition of objects en vision artificial :Application à pedestrian recognition,** 2010.

20. M. D. Youcef, **Deep Learning for image classification**, 2017.

21. Mabah IDOUI and Ahmed HIMEUR, **Image by networks of convolutional neurons (CNN)**, 2019-2020

22. M. M. Zakaria**, Image classification with convolutional neural networks**, 2017.

23. O. Horiya, M. Asma**, Unsupervised classification: Application of k-means**, 2014.

24. S. Bédard-Venne, **Artificial neural network and application image classification**,2018.

25. S. Nebti**, Handwritten Character Recognition using Collective Intelligence**, 2013.

26. Stanislas Lauly**, Exploring autoencoder-based neural networks in the data modelling framework** ,2016

27. Samia SNOUSSI MADDOURI et al, **Segmentation of Arab bank cheques**, 1002, Tunis

28. SAIDI Mohamed and BAKOU Ramande, **Automatic detection of Covid-19 on radiographic images using deep learning**, 2021

29. Z.H. Mamar, **Analyse Temps-Échelle et Reconnaissance des Formes pour le diagnostic du Système de Guidage d'un Tramway sur Pneumatiques**, 2008.

IV. Webography

30. https://moov.ai/fr/blog/deep-learning-avec-google-colab/,Novembre , November2021

31. https://fr.wikipedia.org/wiki/Python_(language), November2021

32. https://fr.wikipedia.org/wiki/NumPy, November2021

33. https://fr.wikipedia.org/wiki/Matplotlib#:~:text=Matplotlib%20est%20une%20biblioth%C3%A8que%20du,calcul%20scientific%20NumPy%20and%20SciPy. November2021

34. https://openclassrooms.com/fr/courses/4452741-decouvrez-les-librairies-python-pour-la-data-science/5559011-make-great-graphics-with-seaborn, November2021

35. https://datafranca.org/wiki/Base_de_donn%C3%A9es_MNIST, November2021

TABLE OF CONTENTS

MIX
Papier aus verantwortungsvollen Quellen
Paper from responsible sources
FSC® C105338

Printed by Books on Demand GmbH, Norderstedt / Germany